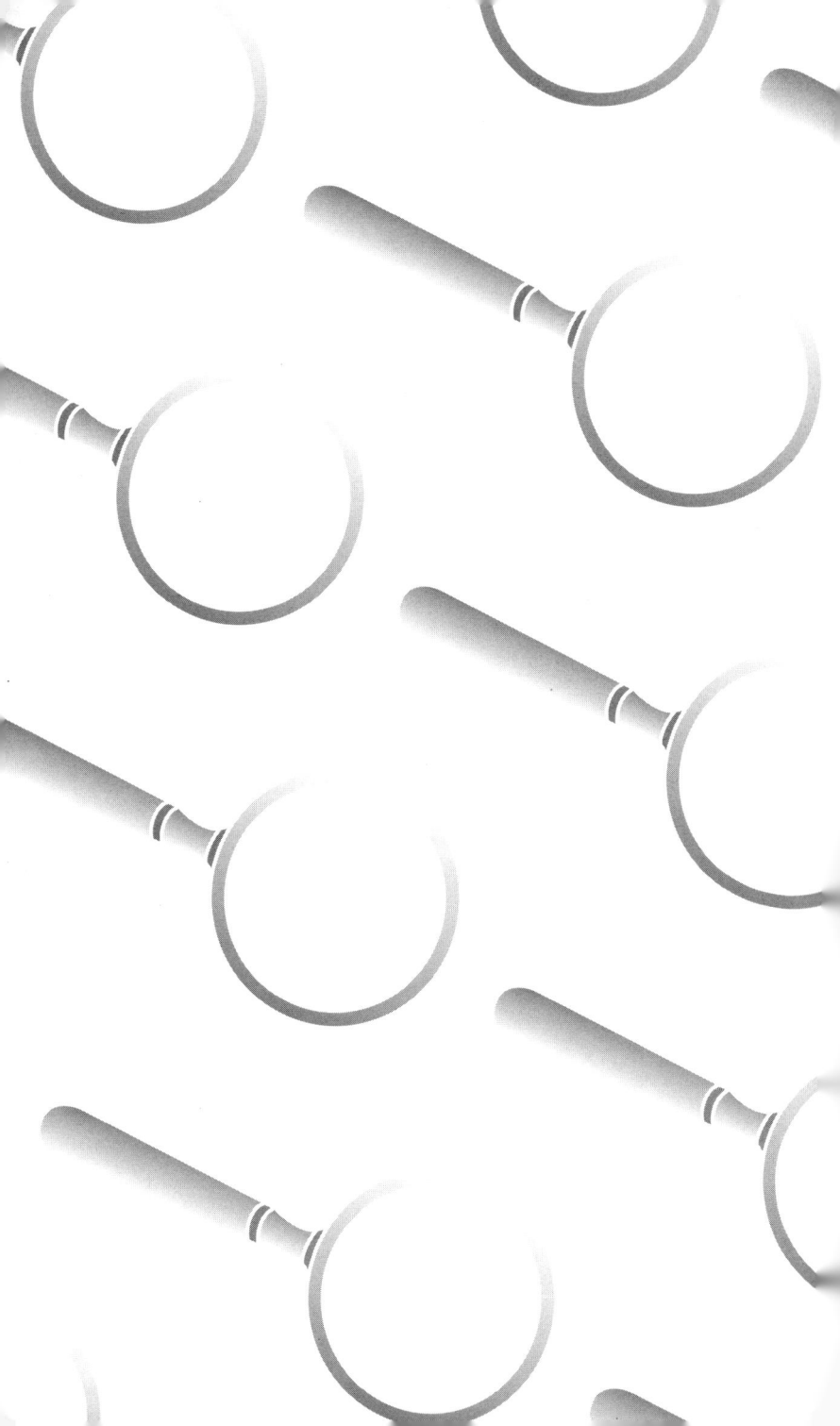

CONTENTS

School was out for the day, and Toad and I were retrieving the briefcase we had stashed in some bushes early that morning.

"Here comes Trudy. Hurry, Toad, ditch it!"

"Why bother? She wouldn't know microfilm from plastic wrap. Don't you worry, Matt, I'll take care of it."

"Hey, guys. What have you got there?" Trudy asked.

"Nothing," said Toad, "just my dad's old briefcase."

"I thought your dad was a doctor."

"He is," Toad replied.

"Then why does his briefcase have 'Top Secret' written on it?"

"He bought it at a garage sale," I said. "A spy must have had it."

Trudy laughed. "You know what I think?"

"I don't really want to know," I said.

She went on anyway. "I think you guys are playing spies and that you have some microfilm in there."

I looked at Toad. "Plastic wrap, huh?"

Trudy was still grinning. "Which one of you is 007? Is it you, Matt?"

"No, not James Bond!"

"Then what *do* you pretend?"

I looked at Toad. Somehow, Trudy's question made me feel like a little kid.

"We don't pretend!" I answered. "And, besides, it's none of your business what we do. Why don't you go and play with the rest of the girls and leave us alone?"

It was mean of me to tell her to go and play with the other girls. I knew none of the girls in our class would have anything to do with Trudy. She had always been a loner. I couldn't remember when she had even one friend. Of course, that must have been the way she wanted it, because she never went out of her way to be nice to any of us.

Ignoring my remark, Trudy said, "Let's see what you've got in there."

"No way!" Toad said, holding the briefcase close to his chest.

"Bet you don't have any plastic explosive in there," Trudy challenged.

Toad and I looked at each other. We'd never thought of plastic explosive!

"Of course we do," I lied. "How do you know about stuff like that?" I asked.

She rolled her eyes. "I live and breathe spy stuff. I bet I've read every book ever written about spies. And I've seen all the James Bond films. Have you?"

"No," Toad said. "We play by our own rules. We think up our own stuff. We don't have to copy films." He almost spat out the word "films".

Trudy didn't say anything. She seemed to be having an argument with herself, then she looked at both of us.

"Can I trust you guys?"

"Depends," I said. I wasn't sure I wanted Trudy telling me any secrets.

"You can trust *me*," Toad said, giving me a wink and a nudge. Toad was my best friend. His real name was Walter, but everyone – except his mother – called him Toad, because he collected frogs and toads. He had three aquariums set up at home, and each one held two or three of the slimy little creatures. I couldn't understand what he liked about them, but he was my friend, so it didn't really matter.

"Well," Trudy began slowly. "I saved my pocket money for months and months and bought a *camera watch!*"

She was so excited that I got the shivers. Her eyes were shining, as though it was something really special.

"So?" I said.

"Just think of the shots you could get if no one knows you have a camera, Matt." Trudy's face broke in a big grin. "I got one of Todd Hunt picking his nose."

Toad and I cracked up. "Chicken Legs Hunt?" I said. "I just have to see this."

"It's at home. I'll let you see it on one condition."

"What's that?" Toad asked.

"You let me play spies with you."

"Forget it," I said flatly. There was no way in the world I'd invite anyone, much less a girl, much less *Gertrude Cooper*, to play spies with Toad and me.

"Maybe we should, Matt," Toad said.

"Look, why do we need to see pictures of Chicken Legs Hunt picking his nose? We can see that any day."

"Yeah, but..." For some reason Toad was still considering Trudy's offer. "Trudy, I need to talk to Matt alone for a minute or two," he said finally.

"OK. You guys go ahead and talk. I'll be over by the bike rack if you're still interested," she said, walking away.

"Listen, Matt," Toad began, "I know you think Trudy's weird, but I think you're forgetting what we could do with that camera watch. I have two words for you: Megan Anderson!"

He had a point. I had been in awe of Megan Anderson for two years. I would love to have her picture. And a camera watch would save me a lot of embarrassment.

"And don't forget about blackmail," Toad continued. "The possibilities are endless."

"You're right," I agreed. "But that doesn't mean Trudy has to be with us all the time. We'll include her sometimes, but not very often. Is that OK?"

"That's OK by me. Let's go."

Trudy was leaning against the bike rack. She looked as if she didn't care whether we turned up or not.

"Well?" she asked.

"OK, you're in. But we get a turn with your camera watch sometimes, too," Toad said.

"That's fair enough. But you have to pay for your own film."

The three of us went off down the street.

I felt weird walking down the street with Trudy. I never thought I cared what other people thought of me, but I found myself wondering how I'd feel if Megan Anderson saw me. I scrunched down as far as I could.

"Something wrong, Matt?" Toad asked.

I glared at him, then decided I'd better stand up straight. Otherwise, I'd end up looking like Quasimodo.

Chapter 2

Trudy made us wait for her outside her garage.

"I don't want my mum to see you guys," she said. "If she does, she'll try to invite you both to dinner or something like that. So wait here."

That was fine by me.

"That's got to be hard," Toad said when she had gone into her house.

"What?"

"Not having any friends."

"Perhaps she's got a dog."

Toad just looked at me and shook his head.

"Here it is," Trudy said, coming around the side of the garage. She had her backpack on, and was holding out her arm with the watch.

"Looks like any other digital watch to me," I said, noting the black plastic strap and the black face showing 4:17.

"That's what makes it so neat," she said, unstrapping the watch. "Look."

She held the watch up sideways and pushed a button I thought would reveal the date but, instead, a tiny viewfinder popped up.

"You just put your arm up to your face with the back of your hand against your nose, then pop the viewfinder and snap the picture with your other hand. It's really simple."

I was fascinated. "How much did it cost?"

"Seventy-five dollars."

"Wow! Your family must be rich."

"No. It took me eight months to save that much. It was all my birthday money *and* my pocket money."

"It even has the right time," Toad observed.

"What did you expect?" Trudy said. "This isn't a toy. Real spies use things like this!"

"Is there film in it?" I asked.

"No. I have only one more roll. I have to order some. It's expensive to develop."

"Can we see some of your pictures?"

Trudy took her backpack off and took out an envelope with tiny pictures in it.

Toad hooted and I laughed when I found the one of Chicken Legs Hunt picking his nose. There was a shot of Jeremy Phillips sticking his tongue out, and one of... well, the picture was of Nicole Green, but Megan Anderson was visible to one side of her. She always looks so *nice*, I thought. Her hair looked soft and her eyes sparkled.

"Look, Matt." Toad was pressing a blob of something in his hands.

"What's that?" I reluctantly handed the pictures back to Trudy and accepted the blob.

"Plastic explosive," Trudy answered.

"Plastic explosive!" I screamed, tossing the blob into the street and running like mad.

"It's not real," Trudy called after me. "Only the camera is real."

I felt really stupid.

"What's in there? All your spy stuff?" Toad asked, pointing at Trudy's backpack.

"Yes. I thought I'd show you what I have and we could compare," she answered.

Besides her camera watch and plastic explosive, she had an encoder kit (complete with codes), dark glasses, a pair of binoculars, a miniature tape recorder, and a wig.

"What's the wig for?" I asked.

"For disguise, of course."

"Pretty impressive," Toad said.

"You can see I'm serious about this," she said. "That's why I have another picture to show you." She fumbled in her backpack.

The picture she pulled out was wrinkled from a lot of handling.

"What *is* this?" Toad asked.

"Just some building," I said.

"No, it's not just *any* building," Trudy said. "It's the Axion building."

"So?" I said, rolling my eyes.

"So, it's the think-tank for the Axion Satellite Corporation. It's a top-secret plant and I'm going to break in."

Chapter 3

"You have to admit she's got guts," Toad said as we walked home. "I never even knew that building was anything special."

"Yeah, much less a plant that's top secret. I'd love to get in there."

"So, what do you think of Trudy now?" Toad asked.

"I think she's smarter than I thought she was," I said as we reached the place in the road where I went one way and Toad went the other. "See you tomorrow. Hey, Toad?"

"Yeah?"

"Do you still have the stink bomb?"

"Yeah, why?"

"Bring it to school, tomorrow. Maybe we can have some fun."

Mrs Larson was looking at me. She's *always* looking at me, just waiting for me to do something wrong so she can give me a detention. But, she's not going to get me today.

"Matt!" Toad whispered behind me.

Mrs Larson finally unlocked her eyes from my face.

I bent sideways in my chair as if I was getting something from inside my desk.

"What?" I whispered crossly. Toad never got into trouble. I did.

"Look at this," he said, tossing me a folded piece of paper.

I opened my maths book and slowly unfolded the paper.

It was a picture of Mrs Larson, drawn to perfection, except that Mrs Larson's hair was high above her head. There was a note next to it: "After seeing Trudy's wig yesterday, I decided Mrs Larson must have one, too!"

A wig! Wow!

I squinted around Nicole Green's head at Mrs Larson. No wonder her hair always looked so perfect – she could take it off every day after school! I started laughing. I couldn't help it. The picture I got in my mind of a bald Mrs Larson was so funny.

"We would *all* enjoy a good laugh, Matthew. Share your thoughts with the rest of the class, please."

"Oh, it's nothing," I stammered, turning pages in my maths book.

"It's *something*, all right," Mrs Larson said. "Especially since we're studying the American Civil War and you're up to your eyes in maths."

The whole class laughed. Even Toad. I could hear his "hee, hee, hee," coming up the aisle behind me.

"Uh, sorry about that," I said, stashing away Toad's drawing in my maths book. I grabbed my history book and glared at Toad. He shrugged, still smiling.

"As I started to say," Mrs Larson said, opening her book, "there were spies during the Civil War just as there are spies today."

Spies! I sat straight up in my desk and looked at Mrs Larson.

"The Confederate Army had their spies and the Union Army had theirs," she continued.

Now *this* was interesting.

"It was much easier to infiltrate the enemy camp in those days, of course. Simply wearing the proper uniform allowed you free access. Not like today. There's simply no way a spy could infiltrate the Axion Satellite Corporation, for instance," she said.

I felt my hand creep up as sweat appeared on my upper lip. "How can you be sure?" I asked, knowing she had to be wrong. Spies could get in anywhere.

"I know because my husband is a scientist, and he works at Axion."

"But spies have ways to get in. They can get in anywhere."

"Not at Axion. I saw that building when it was under construction. The walls are made of concrete, and they're more than a metre thick. And there are no windows."

"But I bet they could just walk in the front door," I said, convinced it wasn't a big deal.

"You've been watching too many films. There's *no way* spies can get inside Axion."

Want to bet? I thought. Then it occurred to me. Maybe we could go on a field trip to Axion and see for ourselves!

"Could your husband show us around? Could we go on a class field trip?"

The whole class jumped in.

"Yes, oh *please*, Mrs Larson?"

"That would be *really* great!"

"Do you think they would let us in?"

"We're not spies or anything."

"*Please*?"

"I don't know." She frowned. "Maybe... I'll ask Mr Larson tonight," she added, smiling. "It *would* be fun, wouldn't it?"

Chapter 4

On the day of our field trip, I pulled on some jeans and a T-shirt, gobbled a bowl of cereal, and ran down the road to meet Toad.

He had our briefcase, and we sat down under the big elm on the front lawn at school to go through our stuff.

Toad made an inventory. "Tape recorder, binoculars, stink bomb... oh yeah, we didn't use that at school. One of these days we..."

"Good," I said. "That's it, except for our top-secret files. Do you think we should put them in?"

"Might as well," Toad said. "Let's go." The whole class was there, excited and ready to go. I could tell that most of the kids couldn't have cared less about going to the Axion plant. They were just glad to be able to get out of school work for a few hours.

Not so with Toad and Trudy and me. The three of us were so excited we could hardly see straight. Of course, Toad and I went out of our way not to sit anywhere near Trudy on the bus, but she managed to sit right behind us and kept chattering all the way to Axion.

"Do you think we'll recognize a spy if we see one?" she asked. "Should I take in my plastic explosive? Maybe I should take my backpack with all my stuff. What do you guys think?"

I hated to admit it, but I was wondering the same thing about our briefcase.

"I doubt if they'll let us bring in anything," Toad said. "I hear they're really strict about that sort of thing. Do you have film in your camera watch?"

"Yes. I loaded it this morning."

"Well, you never know. There may be something to photograph."

I kicked our briefcase under the seat.

Mr Larson met us outside the building. I expected him to be short like Mrs Larson, but he was tall and skinny. He was also in a wheelchair.

He pulled up to the bus and introduced himself, then said, "You'll have to pass through a security check, so please leave all your belongings on the bus. No spy cameras or recording devices," he said, then laughed. "I'm kidding. I know you kids wouldn't have spy cameras or tape recorders."

I nudged Toad and heard Trudy practically choke behind me.

"I'll escort you through the security check and into the main foyer. We have a special visitors' centre. You'll be taken there for a briefing. This is the first time we've had children here. Usually it's someone from the government. So you can see you're in good company."

A briefing! I thought. Wow! Just like they do in the films.

Going through the security check was scary. There were two guards, and they weren't laughing. They looked us over very carefully. They even looked through Mrs Larson's handbag! I was glad we'd left the briefcase on the bus.

As we crossed the parking area, Mr Larson kept talking. "Just last week we found a briefcase in the foyer with no identification. We couldn't work out who it belonged to, so we took it out there," he pointed to a concrete cylinder in an open field next to the parking area. "Then, we blew it up. Now, children, we wouldn't want that to happen to your backpacks or school books, would we?" He laughed loudly.

Toad and I looked at each other. I gulped.

"They mean business," I whispered.

When we got to the foyer, I was really disappointed. It looked like any other foyer. Lots of artificial trees and plants surrounded the receptionist's desk on one side, and double doors led to a conference room on the other side. And – now this was different! – at the far end of the foyer, a guard stood in front of a steel door that was firmly closed. Next to the door was a panel about thirty-centimetres square. I wondered what it was for.

Then, I saw a tall, skinny man with a thin face. He was wearing a white uniform with MooTown Dairy on the back, and pushing a cart with milk, ice cream, and yogurt down the hall. He smiled at us, showing long teeth.

Mr Larson led our group towards the visitors' centre. I knew that once we were inside, we wouldn't have a chance of discovering anything exciting.

I quickly raised my hand. "Mr Larson? What's the panel next to the steel door for?"

"Glad you asked. Come over here."

The whole class followed him obediently.

"This door leads to the security area. No one can get through this door without a security card. This is what the card looks like," he said, holding his up. "You'll notice my picture is on the card. The security guard will look at my picture to be sure the card is mine. When he's convinced I have a right to be here, he hands the card back and I run it through this magnetic lock. Hey presto! The door opens."

As he spoke, the steel door swung open and out stepped a young man. He was younger than Mr Larson, that is.

"Now, we really didn't plan this," Mr Larson said. "This is my colleague, Charlie Brown, the cleverest man I know. How about that name, kids? Charlie Brown." He laughed.

Mr Brown smiled broadly. "I've been living down that name all my life. Are you all having fun?" he asked, changing the subject.

"Yeah, it's great."

"This place is cool!"

"Can we see some satellites?"

"Of course. Mr Larson is going to take you into the visitors' centre and show you a video about one of our satellites from the time it's put into the cargo bay of the space shuttle until it's deployed, or kicked out into space like a frisbee."

While he was talking, I noticed a strange look flicker across Mr Brown's face when he saw the man making the dairy delivery walk past.

As the class moved across the foyer, Toad hung back.

"What's up?" I whispered.

"Let's see how long it takes them to find us," he whispered back.

We drifted to the end of the group and, instead of going into the visitors' centre, we backed down the hall and ducked into the conference room. It was a large room, with a long table in the middle.

"We did it! We really did it!" Toad said. "We disappeared in a security complex!"

"Now, if we could just get through that steel door," I said.

"No way. I think Mrs Larson's right about no one being able to break into this place," Toad said.

Just then the door opened a crack. We stood there, glued to the floor, not daring to breathe.

The door opened wider.

"Trudy!" I whispered. "What do you think you're doing?"

"Following you guys." She stopped suddenly. Then I heard voices coming closer.

"Hide!" I whispered.

Trudy just stood there.

"Come on!" I said, grabbing her hand and pulling her into a cupboard next to the door.

My whispered instructions were cut off as the door to the conference room was pushed open. I held my breath and pressed in next to Toad and Trudy.

"I told you *never* to contact me here! Are you mad? This could blow the whole operation!"

The cupboard door was open just enough for me to see Charlie Brown!

Chapter 5

"I had to contact you," another man's voice said. "My people are demanding the plans by noon, today. I have less than two hours to get them there."

I couldn't see the other person, but Charlie Brown was holding out two mechanical pencils. "The plans are on microfilm rolled up in the lead compartment of this pencil," Charlie Brown said. "See?" He held up one of the mechanical pencils.

I nudged Trudy and pointed to her wrist. I'd never seen her eyes so big before! She nodded and put her camera watch up to her eye and snapped. The camera was soundless.

"Do you see the difference between this pencil and a company pencil?" Mr Brown asked, holding up the other pencil.

"No," the other voice answered.

"Pay attention, you fool!" Mr Brown obviously didn't think much of the man.

I tried to gently push the door open a little further, so I could see who Charlie Brown was speaking to, but I was afraid the door would squeak, so I stopped.

"The one with the plans has a red line around the top," Mr Brown said.

Footsteps approached the conference room. "Take them, you fool!" Mr Brown turned towards the door, and I heard the other man duck behind the table.

The door banged open and I recognized Chicken Legs Hunt's voice.

"Excuse me. Have you seen some kids? We've lost some of them."

"They're not in here," Mr Brown said, all smiles. "Why don't you look out by the receptionist's desk where all the trees and plants are? It's like a jungle out there. They might be hiding."

"Thanks," Chicken Legs Hunt said. Mr Brown walked out with him.

When the door closed, the other man came out from behind the table. I got a good look at him and Trudy took his picture. It was the man making the dairy delivery.

He stopped in front of the door and pulled out both of the pencils. He studied them closely, then smiled, revealing his long teeth. He opened the door a crack, peered out, and left the conference room.

I let out a big breath I didn't even realize I had been holding and stepped out of the cupboard. My legs were all rubbery.

Trudy stepped out, putting her hand on my shoulder to steady herself and practically knocked me over.

"Take it easy," I said, when I could breathe again.

Toad peeked out the door into the foyer. After a moment, he closed it and said, "All clear. Did you see that man?"

"Who, Low Fat?" I shivered. "That man gave me the creeps even when I thought all he did was deliver milk."

"Why are you guys just standing here?" Trudy asked. "Let's go and tell Mr Larson that his friend's a spy."

Toad and I looked at each other. "Watch the door," I said to Trudy.

"Why?"

"To see where Low Fat went," I told her.

When Trudy went to the door, I said, "What do you think, Toad? Should we try to talk to Mr Larson?"

"Let's see if we can find Low Fat first and get those pencils from him. He wouldn't do anything to us with all these guards around."

"Can you see Low Fat?" I called to Trudy.

"He just went out the front door. And he was in a big hurry," she called back.

"There goes that idea," Toad muttered. "We'd better try to sneak into the visitors' centre without being noticed."

The videotape of the space-shuttle crew and the Axion satellite was still playing, so we sat down quietly in the darkened room. It was just my luck to sit next to Chicken Legs Hunt.

"Hey, where've you guys been? I've been looking everywhere," he whispered.

"We've been spying on spies," I answered.

"Sure. And pigs might fly," he said.

I noticed Mr Larson sitting to the side, watching the video. I leaned down to catch Toad's eye, but he was one step ahead of me. He stood and motioned for me to follow him.

"Mr Larson? Could we talk to you for a minute?" Toad asked politely.

"Of course, boys. What is it?"

"It's, uh, a bit private. Could we go out to the foyer?"

He looked at Toad, then at me. Finally, he nodded and we followed him out.

Toad and I looked around to be sure no one else could hear us.

"It's about Mr Brown," Toad began.

There was a shuffling noise behind us and we both spun around.

"Trudy!"

"Why did you leave me behind? I'm in this just as much as you two." Her eyes were flashing angry sparks. Then she turned her attention to Mr Larson.

"Did they tell you that your friend Mr Brown is a spy? Did they tell you we saw him pass top-secret information to that milk-delivery person?"

Mr Larson shook his head. "All right, calm down. You kids have overactive imaginations. Do you want to start at the beginning and tell me what this is all about?"

"Well," I said. "We were all in the conference room and…"

"Go on," Mr Larson said to me.

"We heard voices, so we hid in the cupboard," I continued. "We could see Mr Brown through the open door and he was angry with the other man for coming here. But the other man said he had to come because 'his people' wanted the plans by noon, today."

"Just how do you know he's a spy?" Mr Larson asked.

"Well, Mr Brown gave him two mechanical pencils and told him that the microfilm was rolled up in the lead compartment of the one with the red line around the top," I finished breathlessly.

Mr Larson held up a box I hadn't even seen him carrying, opened it, and took out a mechanical pencil.

"Is this the type of pencil?" he asked.

"Yes, that's it!" Toad replied.

"We have *thousands* of these pencils. We give them away all the time. I have this box to give to your class. Let's open a pencil and see if it's possible to hide microfilm in it," he said, pulling a pencil apart. He dumped out the lead and held up the empty cylinder.

"I want you to look closely at this," he said. "I told you we give away thousands of these pencils. But the company isn't overly generous. These are specially made with very small lead compartments, only large enough for three tiny sticks of lead so that it doesn't cost Axion too much money. There's no room in here for microfilm, or anything else."

"But the one with the microfilm had a red line around the top," Trudy objected.

"Did it look exactly like this?" Mr Larson asked, holding up the company pencil again.

"Except for the red line," Trudy answered.

"If it was the same size as this, it's impossible. Red line or not, there's no room inside for anything."

"But..." I started.

"There's something else you kids should know," Mr Larson continued. "I told you

41

before that Charlie Brown is the cleverest man I know, and he's a colleague. We're also good friends. He comes to my home for dinner at least once a week. We go fishing together. We play cards together. He's the most loyal and trustworthy person I've ever known. Charlie Brown is *not* a spy. I've known him for ten years. Now, I want you to get this mad idea out of your heads and stop making accusations that could ruin a good man's life."

Mr Larson looked very stern. He wasn't laughing now. He meant business.

"And another thing," he said. "Don't you dare bother my wife with any of this nonsense. She has enough worries right now and I don't want her upset. I'm going to forget you ever told me this, and I suggest you do the same."

Mr Larson turned and wheeled back into the visitors' centre.

We followed him.

Chapter 6

"Mr Larson probably thinks we dreamt up the whole thing," I said. We were all sitting under the big elm tree on the lawn after school.

"But, we didn't. I know what I saw and heard with my own two eyes and ears," Trudy answered, twirling and tapping her mechanical pencil from Axion.

"Yeah, so do I. But what do you think we can do about it?"

"We could try to find out where Charlie Brown lives," Toad said.

I looked at him and a light bulb flicked on over my head. "Yeah! And *prove* he's a spy!"

"If we proved it, they'd have to believe us," Trudy chirped, her eyes gleaming.

I grabbed a notepad and pencil out of our briefcase.

"OK, let's decide how we're going to do this," I said, preparing to take notes.

"If we could find his house, we could follow him," Toad said.

"How do we find his house?" Trudy asked.

"Start with the telephone book. If he's unlisted, we could always ask Mrs Larson," I said, jotting down notes on the pad.

"No way," Toad said. "She'd tell Mr Larson, then we'd be in really big trouble."

"If we could find out where he lives, we could follow him this weekend," Trudy said. "Maybe even find Low Fat."

Just then I heard giggling and turned to see Nicole Green and Megan Anderson coming down the steps of the school.

Megan looked at me, then she saw Trudy and her face froze. She and Nicole hurried away, heads together, whispering.

My stomach dropped to my toes. I tried to picture what Megan had seen. Toad was sitting next to me on one side and Trudy on the other. But I had been looking at Trudy and I probably looked happy and excited. There's no way Megan could know I was excited about finding Charlie Brown and not about Trudy.

"Hey, Matt," Trudy said.

"What?" I was still watching Megan disappear down the street.

"Let's go and find a telephone book," Trudy continued, standing up. Toad stood up, too.

"Why don't you just get lost," I said nastily.

Trudy looked hurt and just stood there.

Toad looked at me strangely, then said, "Come on, Trudy. He didn't mean it."

I was beyond caring what they did, but I headed towards the shop a street away from school. They followed behind me.

There was a telephone booth in front of the shop. I grabbed the telephone book and turned to the *B*s."Brady, Brooks, Broper..."

"I'm looking for a Charles or C. Brown." My patience was stretched as thin as spaghetti.

"It's easier than that," Toad said. "Look, there's a Charlie Brown listed. It's got to be him."

"What's the address?" asked Trudy.

"311 Maple Street," I said.

"You're sure? That's the street behind my house!" Trudy was practically frothing at the mouth.

"Let's go and have a look," I said, forgetting for a moment how upset I felt.

We were close to Charlie Brown's house when Toad stopped us.

"How are we going to do this?" he asked. "We're not going to ring the bell or anything, are we?"

"Let's just walk past as though we're just walking down the street," I said. "We can try to see in his windows without being too obvious."

"We can't see in the windows unless we go on to the porch," Trudy said. "Of course," she giggled, "we can always play Ring and Run."

"That's not a bad idea," Toad said.

We slowly approached 311 Maple Street. It was a small house with a close-cut lawn.

Toad volunteered to ring the doorbell. Trudy and I hid in the bushes on the neighbour's property. I watched to see if this was really our Charlie Brown.

Toad punched the bell, then raced down the steps and dived into the bushes.

I heard the door slowly open and someone came out on to the porch, but I couldn't quite see from my position. There was a dog barking somewhere in the house, then a familiar voice said, "It's OK, boy. Quiet, now. Must have been some kids playing a trick."

The footsteps turned and went back inside, and the screen door slammed behind them.

We waited a few minutes, then slowly crept out of the bushes.

Trudy had a big grin on her face. "It was our spy!" she said. "It was Charlie Brown!"

"Let's just tell the whole world, why don't we?" I snapped.

We raced down the street. When we turned the corner, I leaned up against an old oak tree. Its canopy of leaves shielded us from the late afternoon sun.

"Let's stop a minute. We're not being chased or anything." I was in a rotten mood, but I didn't care. Megan had seen me with Trudy. And Toad didn't seem to mind.

"What's bugging you, Matt?" he asked.

"You really don't know?"

"Would I ask if I knew?" He looked completely puzzled.

"Forget it," I said to Toad and turned back to look at him. "It's not important..." I stopped in mid-sentence, my mouth hanging open. Walking along the pavement behind Toad was Charlie Brown and a huge dog!

Chapter 7

Toad saw the look on my face and spun around. Trudy stood frozen, her eyes popping.

Charlie Brown stopped beside us. He was holding onto his huge, shaggy grey-and-white dog's lead.

"Have you kids been ringing any doorbells near here?" he asked.

"We..." I croaked. What's the use? He's worked it out.

"No problem," he said, smiling his traitor's smile that made everyone think he's Mr Nice.

"My name is Charlie Brown, and this is my dog, Dudley. I used to do the same kind of things when I was your age. You kids live around here?"

Trudy looked at Toad and me. "Why?"

"I need someone to do me a favour. Someone who lives near by."

"I do," Trudy said. "I live just down the street."

Trudy was a lot braver than I had thought. She was leaving herself wide open, telling him where she lived.

"Great! Do you like dogs?" Charlie Brown asked, smiling.

"I love dogs," Trudy said, then she rolled her eyes. "But Mum says they're too hard to train."

She was watching Charlie Brown's big dog while she talked and he suddenly lunged at her. I held my breath, thinking Trudy was about to be eaten alive. Instead, the dog's huge pink tongue lavished wet licks all over her hands and arms.

Trudy giggled and Charlie Brown laughed.

"Stop it, Dudley! She doesn't need a bath." He pulled on the lead and Dudley sat obediently at his side, but the dog's tail was still wagging.

"What kind of dog is he?" Trudy asked.

"An Old English sheepdog. In fact, he's the reason I was hoping to find someone who lives near here. I have to go away on Saturday and I won't be back until Tuesday. I need someone to feed Dudley and take him for a walk every day while I'm away."

"I'll be glad to do it!" she said, obviously delighted. "But I'll have to ask Mum first."

"Good. I'll give you my address and phone number so your mum can call me." He pulled a pen and a small notebook out of his jacket pocket.

"If Mum says it's OK, I'll come over to your house on Friday evening," Trudy said. "Then, you can show me where everything is."

Good thinking, Trudy! I thought. This way, we could find out about the layout of his house. Besides, there was no sense in letting a spy know exactly where she lived.

"That's fine with me," Charlie Brown said. "Will five dollars a day be enough?" He looked so nice. He certainly had everyone fooled.

Trudy gulped. "Oh yes. But you don't have to pay me. I mean, not unless you want to."

"It's worth it to me to have someone responsible looking after Dudley."

"Can my friends come, too?" she asked.

"Yes, if they like. See you on Friday." He smiled and started jogging down the street.

Dudley kept turning back and looking at us, wagging his tail.

"Can you believe it?" Trudy asked, slumping against the tree.

"I don't think he even realized we were out at Axion," Toad said.

"That dog is huge," I said.

"I love that dog," Trudy said wistfully. "I wish he were mine."

"It doesn't seem right that a creep like Charlie Brown should have such a great dog," Toad said.

My mind wasn't on the dog any more. I had just realized what Trudy's job could mean.

"Listen, you guys. Soon we'll be able to go through Charlie Brown's house. Maybe we'll find something that will prove he's a spy once and for all."

After dinner on Friday, I asked my mum if I could go over to Toad's for a little while.

"Of course you can," she said. "Just be home before it gets dark."

As soon as Toad and I picked up Trudy, we made our way to Charlie Brown's house.

When Trudy knocked on the door, my heart started thumping and my hands got sweaty. Toad was swallowing a lot. Only Trudy didn't seem nervous.

Charlie Brown answered the door with his big smile. "Come in. Dudley's been racing around for the last hour waiting for you."

He led us into a very neat, very plain living room. There were pictures of snowy mountains on the walls and furniture in the usual places.

I don't know what I expected – maybe a few daggers on the wall and a rack for stretching people. But his home looked so *ordinary*.

"I'll just leave the dog food out here on the back porch. You can fill his water bowl with the hose. His lead hangs on a hook by the door," Charlie Brown was saying, showing us where everything was.

But if everything was on the back porch, we wouldn't be getting a key to the house! That meant we wouldn't be able to get in and find any evidence.

Then Trudy spoke. "Mr Brown, what if it rains or we get early snow or something? Wouldn't you want Dudley to be inside the house?"

"Absolutely!" Charlie Brown flashed his sickening smile again. "That's why I have a doggy door." He stepped aside so we could see the flap cut into the side of the house. It was too small for a man to get through, but just right for a dog... or a kid!

Our worries are over, I thought.

Toad's eyes were gleaming. He had worked it out, too.

"Twenty dollars! Imagine getting paid twenty dollars for something you'd gladly do anyway. Wow!" Trudy was bubbling with excitement as we left Charlie Brown's house.

"Know what I'm going to do with it?" she said walking backwards down the street, facing us in the twilight. "I'm going to get that film developed – the pictures we took at Axion."

Toad laughed. "Charlie Brown is paying for the pictures that will some day be used against him in a court of law. That's *really* bizarre!"

"Poetic justice," I said. I had heard that somewhere and liked it.

Chapter 8

We had agreed to meet Trudy at Charlie Brown's house at noon. I was a little late because Saturdays are job days at our house, and no one leaves until everything is done. The wind had blown all the leaves off the trees during the night, and I had to rake them up. It was a huge job.

Toad and Trudy were waiting on Charlie Brown's front porch.

"Where have you been?" Toad said.

"Raking leaves," I mumbled. "Have you seen anything yet?"

"No, we were waiting for you. Let's get going," Trudy said, leading the way.

She pushed the gate open and was knocked over by Dudley, who was wild with excitement. The dog was so happy to see us, he practically wagged himself in two. Trudy laughed and played with him while Toad filled his water bowl. His food bowl was still full. After about fifteen minutes, Dudley calmed down and curled up for a sleep.

The three of us sat on the grass.

"Well? Where do we start?" I asked.

"I think two of us should go into the house and search while one of us looks out for anyone who might be watching," Toad said.

"Who's going to stay out here and keep watch?" I asked, looking at Trudy.

"Oh no, you don't," she said, getting up and stomping over to the doggy door. "You guys wouldn't even be here if it weren't for me. *I'm* going to investigate. There's *no way* I'm going to stay out here!"

There's something about Trudy when she gets mad. Her face gets flushed and her eyes shoot sparks.

"I'll stay out here," I offered.

Toad looked at me as if I'd lost my mind.

"No, it's OK. You two go in and I'll keep watch. I don't mind. Really." I made myself comfortable next to Dudley and watched as Toad, shaking his head in disbelief, followed Trudy.

I started walking around the yard, kicking at blades of grass and imaginary rocks in the well-kept lawn. There were some tomatoes and green beans growing in one corner and I bent to look at them. A green leaf, next to a big tomato, started to move. I bent closer. The leaf moved again. I watched it, fascinated. It wasn't a leaf. It was a fat, squishy tomato worm!

"Yuck!" I said, feeling my face contort into a grimace. "Double yuck."

I backed away but my eyes were riveted to the horn-covered green creature.

A screen door slammed and my head jerked up. The next-door neighbour was standing on her back porch watching me!

"Oh, hi," I said, my voice cracking. "You're probably wondering what I'm doing here."

She kept staring.

"I'm helping my friend take care of Dudley. Here, Dudley," I called, trying to prove to her I wasn't lying.

Dudley pranced over to me and licked my hand, his tail wagging. Good dog!

The woman turned and went back into her house without saying anything.

I breathed a sigh of relief, then it hit me. What if she went in and called the police?

I ran to the door and yanked it open, just as Toad and Trudy were coming out.

"What's wrong?" Toad asked.

"The lady next door saw me. I think she might call the police!"

"Why? Did you do anything wrong?"

"Well, no but..."

Toad sighed. "Relax, Matt. The house is locked and we're in the backyard with Dudley, where we're supposed to be."

He was right. I was worrying about nothing.

"Did you find anything?" I asked.

"Nothing," Trudy said. "That man's really fussy. There isn't so much as a scrap of paper that doesn't belong there."

"Oh no," I said, disappointed. This wasn't going as well as we thought it would. It made sense, though. Charlie Brown would have to be a real beginner to leave evidence lying around his house.

My eyes rested on the tomato plants and a small smile slid across my face.

"Hey, Trudy, come here a minute," I said.

Toad looked at me with a frown. He knew something was up.

"Isn't this a great tomato plant?" I asked.

"It's OK," she said.

"Look at this leaf. Isn't it a pretty colour?" I asked.

Trudy looked at me as if I was nuts, then she examined the "leaf".

"If you've seen one leaf, you've seen them all," she said, then she stopped. I expected her to scream, but she didn't.

"Oh, it's a worm," she said flatly. "I dare you to eat it."

"What?" I couldn't have heard her right.

"I said, I dare you to eat it," Trudy repeated. I could see the challenge in her eyes. Toad sniggered.

I looked at the tomato worm. I thought I could get it down in two gulps, if I could bite it in half. "OK, if that's what you want," I said.

I reached down and plucked the worm from the plant. I tried desperately not to show my disgust. The worm twisted in my fingers, its legs and horns bristling. I kept telling myself it was a mini hot dog, but it didn't look like one. I gagged, then broke out in a cold sweat. I looked at Toad. He grinned and shrugged.

I made a supreme effort, opening my mouth and holding the worm over it. I took a deep breath, then shook my head. I couldn't do it.

Toad was grinning from ear to ear. "Well, better luck next time!" he said, patting me on the back.

Then I noticed Trudy bending low over the tomato plants. Curious, I bent down to see what she was looking at.

There was a small metal ring sticking up through the earth. Trudy tried to pick it up, but it wouldn't move. It was attached to something. She brushed the earth away from the ring, exposing a metal lid. Putting her finger through the ring, she pulled hard and the lid popped open.

All three of us peered into a metal box buried in the ground.

Chapter 9

The box was empty.

"This seems a pretty strange place to bury a box," Toad said.

"Not if it's where you want to keep top-secret material you're planning to sell to the enemy," Trudy observed.

"She may be right, Toad. This is an ideal place to hide papers," I said grudgingly. Trudy was right on top of things, I had to admit.

"If this is where Charlie Brown hides his stuff, then why is it empty?" Toad asked.

He had a point.

"Maybe he took it with him on his trip. I don't know. But I *do* know we have to keep an eye on this box. We should check it every week," Trudy said.

"And how are we going to do that?" I sneered.

"I, for one, can come over any time to play with Dudley," Trudy answered, her nose in the air.

"Well, good for you," I said, just as snooty as I could be.

Toad stepped in. "Cut it out, you two. Trudy's right. We'll have to check this box as often as we can. It doesn't do any good for you two to fight."

I walked around the yard, looking over the fence at the houses on the next street.

"Trudy, where do you live?" I asked.

"Four houses down. See the backyard with the clothesline? That's mine. Why?"

"Do you think you could see Charlie Brown's backyard from your window?"

"Yeah, I know I can. I've already checked. I... I watch Dudley," she said, embarrassed.

"You could watch out to see if Charlie Brown buries anything," Toad said.

"I'll try. But I can't see the whole backyard. Just a small part of it."

"We'll just have to make excuses to play with Dudley and check it every week," Toad said. "Let's go."

"Pssst," Toad whispered from two desks behind me.

I ducked my head down and turned towards him. "What?"

He silently rolled a wad of paper up the aisle and I grabbed it. I started unwrapping it, curious about the method Toad had used to pass the note. Usually, we put them in a book and give it to Chicken Legs Hunt, who sits between us and passes it on. I spread the paper out on my desk, completely baffled. It said, "Matt + Megan!"

I quickly folded the note up, but not quite quickly enough.

"I'll take that," Mrs Larson said.

"Please, Mrs Larson. It really isn't anything," I said, scrunching up the note. My neck felt hot and I knew my face was red.

"Hand it over, young man." She wasn't in a very good mood.

I gave her the note.

She went back to her desk, sat down and unfolded the paper.

I felt that my heart would stop any minute now and it would be all over. I hoped Toad would be sorry for the rest of his life because he'd caused my death.

The rest of the class was holding its breath. Mrs Larson looked up at me, then jotted something in her book. She never said a word. We all sighed and got back to work.

About ten minutes later I heard another "Pssst!" from behind me.

No way, I thought.

"Pssst, Matt!"

I didn't even look around this time. I just shook my head.

"Pssst!" Toad was getting louder.

Mrs Larson was writing on the board with her back to us, so I knew she couldn't tell what was going on.

Maybe I should see what he wants, I thought, ducking down next to my desk.

He carefully rolled another wad of paper towards me and I grabbed it.

Mrs Larson was still writing on the board.

This time the paper said, "Can you get a chicken heart?"

Chicken heart! I spun around and looked at Toad. "Are you mad?" I mouthed.

Toad's eyes suddenly got very big and I knew exactly what was coming before I even turned around.

Mrs Larson's cheeks were quivering like marshmallows, she was so mad. "Report for a detention after school, young man. Every day this week!"

Toad and Trudy were waiting for me when I got out of school at four-thirty that afternoon.

Before I could say anything, Toad said, "I'm really sorry, Matt. I didn't really think she'd catch us the second time."

"What do you mean, *us?*" I growled. I was mad and Toad knew it. "Did you get a detention? No, I got a detention. Some friend!"

"Look, before you become unglued, listen to this," Toad said.

Trudy's eyes were bright as she started talking. "I was reading this neat book about dog training," she said. "And it explained ways to get a dog to do what you want it to do."

"What are you talking about?" Trudy really baffled me.

"It's pretty simple, Matt," Toad said.

I snarled at him and he shut up.

"Dogs like chicken hearts," Trudy continued. "If we give Dudley lots of treats like that, he'll like us more, and we can get him on our side."

"He seems to like us quite a lot, already," I said scornfully. "Besides, I've read that chicken bones are bad for dogs."

"She's not talking about chicken *bones*, Matt," observed Toad.

"No, Toad," I sneered.

"The point is to have the dog obey *us*, not Charlie Brown," Trudy said, grabbing my arm. "It's worth a try, don't you think? Besides, Mum said if I was serious about having a dog I should read a book about training, and she might let me have one."

I looked at her hand as if it were a worm. After spending the last hour washing chalkboards, I wasn't sure I wanted to try out anything else. But it *did* sound interesting. "It can't hurt, I suppose. Let's do it."

"Great!" Toad said. "Since your mum cooks chicken every week, you can get the heart, Matt, OK?"

"Why don't you get it?" I was getting tired of being responsible for everything.

"Come on, Matt. You know the only kind of chicken my mum ever cooks is in one of those frozen dinners. They don't put the hearts in those things."

He had a point.

"All right. I'll bring it to school when I get it. And I'll bring the liver and gizzard, too. Now, if we're going to see Dudley, we'd better hurry. It'll be dark soon."

Dudley was so excited to see us he nearly knocked us all down. Trudy played with him while Toad filled his water and food bowls.

All of a sudden, Dudley stopped dead in his tracks and cocked his head to one side.

Toad and I looked at each other, then crept over to the fence. We could see between the slats, and we kept our heads down so we wouldn't be seen from the other side. Trudy kept her arms around Dudley to keep him still.

I heard a van door slide open and heavy footsteps go up the path to the front door, but I couldn't see who it was. The doorbell rang and rang, then someone pounded on the door. After a few minutes, the footsteps went back to the van.

Toad crept along the fence until he was at the corner where the van was parked. He slowly raised his head above the fence, then the van door slammed closed and the engine roared into life.

Toad sunk down and turned to me. His face was white. "It was Low Fat," he whispered.

Chapter 10

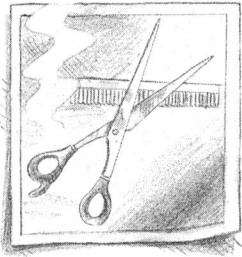

"Quick, you guys! Try to get his licence number," Trudy said, clambering over the fence.

"It's too late. He's already gone around the corner," I said, sitting down on the grass. "All we really know is that he drives a brand-new white van."

"Big deal," Toad said, sitting next to me.

"What's the matter with you two?" Trudy was excited. "Why are you giving up so easily? It's another lead. There can't be that many white vans in this area."

Dudley was lying down now, half asleep, and Trudy was next to him. In the late afternoon sunlight her hair was shiny and there was a flush on her cheeks. She looked OK. Maybe my mum was right. She was always saying that beauty comes from the inside. You just needed to get to know someone.

What was I thinking? All that chalk dust must have gone straight to my brain.

The rest of the week was a pain. Charlie Brown came home on Tuesday and paid Trudy her twenty dollars. While I emptied rubbish bins and cleaned classrooms every afternoon, Trudy and Toad spent their time after school looking for Low Fat's white van.

Mum cooked chicken on Thursday night, and she didn't notice that I took the little bag with all the organs out of the rubbish and put it in a sandwich bag to take to school on Friday.

Mrs Larson was called out of the room that morning, so Toad, Trudy, and I examined the contents of the bag, trying to work out what was what. We had pretty much decided by the time Mrs Larson came back, so I shoved the bag back into my desk.

I really thought things had improved that day, especially when Toad invited me to stay at his house that night.

But my mum didn't think I'd been punished enough, so she wouldn't let me go. Instead, I was "allowed" to go to the shop for her.

As I walked down the aisles looking for barbecue sauce, I heard a familiar laugh.

Mr Larson! I sneaked around the corner of the tinned-soup aisle and saw Mr Larson talking to Charlie Brown.

I couldn't hear what they were saying, so I quietly went down the tinned-fruit aisle on the other side of them and put my ear between two tins of pineapple.

"I just got back from Washington on Tuesday, but I've been working on some priority stuff in the lab. That's why I haven't seen you," Charlie Brown said.

"I've been so worried about Mandy, I probably wouldn't have noticed if you'd been there," Mr Larson answered.

Mandy? I knew that had to be Mrs Larson, but why was he worried?

"How is she?" Charlie Brown asked.

"The new medicine really makes her tired, but she won't take any time off school. It's hard for her to handle those kids. Most of them are pretty good, but there are a couple..."

"I know just what you mean," Charlie Brown said, nodding.

"Speaking of kids," Mr Larson said. "I forgot to tell you what some of them said to me the day Mandy brought them to Axion." He started laughing. "They said you were a *spy*!"

"A spy?" Charlie Brown started laughing, too. "Which kids? What did they look like?" he asked between gasps of laughter.

"Young man, will you please get your ear out of the pineapple so I can do my shopping?" a skinny woman with a baby asked.

I moved aside reluctantly, wanting desperately to hear Mr Larson's reply. Just then the baby started screaming, and whatever Mr Larson said was lost.

"It's all right, Roger." The woman patted the baby, then turned to me. "Roger has earache. The pain starts without warning. He can't help crying."

"That's all right," I said. What was I supposed to do about Roger and his earache?

When the woman and Roger moved away, I heard the two men's voices growing fainter as they moved down the aisle.

I had to get home and phone Toad!

"Where's the barbecue sauce?" Mum asked.

"I forgot it."

"You forgot the only thing I sent you to the shop for?" Her eyes were huge and her eyebrows disappeared somewhere in her hair.

"I'll go back," I said, heading for the door.

"No! No, you stay right here," my mum said, grabbing my arm. "You might forget to come home at all. I'll go." She got her handbag and the car keys and was gone.

"Hey, Toad, guess what?" I said when Toad answered the phone.

"What?"

"Charlie Brown knows we're on to him. We could be in big trouble." I told him what I had heard in the shop.

"I wish we knew if he knows it's us or not," Toad said. He sounded worried.

"Me, too. We'll just have to treat it like he *does* know, that's all."

"What about Trudy? She plans to go and play with Dudley on Sunday and take him for a walk. Maybe she shouldn't go," Toad said.

I thought about that for a minute. "Suppose Mr Larson didn't tell him it was us. It wouldn't look good if Trudy doesn't go over there. He might start getting really suspicious."

"I suppose so. It might be better if the three of us weren't seen together, though."

"You're right." I agreed.

"I'll call Trudy. See you, Matt."

On Saturday, my mum insisted that I get my hair cut. As I rode my bike to the barbers, I wondered what Toad was doing. It was going to be hard not to hang around with him all day.

I parked my bike in front of the barbers, went in, and sat down to wait. The barber, Mr Irwin, and the customer whose hair he had just started cutting both had their backs to me.

I was feeling pretty bored by the time Mr Irwin turned his customer around and gave him a big mirror so he could see the back of his head. But when I glanced up, my mouth fell open. Mr Irwin's customer was Low Fat!

"You're next, Matt, I won't be a moment," Mr Irwin said, smiling.

"No, I have to go. I'll come back later. Besides, I don't really need a haircut. My mum does. I mean, she thinks I do, but I don't." I was backing out of the shop, my eyes glued to Low Fat, who was smiling a big, toothy smile.

"If you like, I'll give you a haircut." Low Fat said, pretending his fingers were scissors and making cutting motions next to his head.

"It's OK," I said, trying to smile.

"What do you want to be when you grow up?" he asked.

"I... I don't know," I said.

"Do you study hard?"

"Oh yes. Yes, I do."

"That's good. You keep working hard and grow up to be a scientist," Low Fat nodded.

"Are you a scientist?" I asked.

"No, but I wish I were. I just work for a dairy company, but I know a scientist, and he makes a lot of money."

Yeah, I bet, I thought. Your scientist is a dirty spy who sells secrets to the highest bidder.

"Well, I've got to go. See you," I said, and ran out the door.

As I pedalled away, I noticed the white van parked around the corner. The licence plate was right in front of me – XRAT9.

At half past ten that night, our phone rang. My mum jumped up and said, "Somebody's died. No one calls after ten o'clock unless somebody's died. Hello? Hello?"

She didn't say anything for a minute, then she handed the phone to me. She was still mad at me for forgetting to get a haircut.

It was Trudy.

"Why are you phoning so late?" I asked, watching my mum glare at me as she made her way back to her room.

"He's out there with a torch, Matt," Trudy whispered excitedly. "I can see Charlie Brown from my window. I can't see what he's doing, but I know he's over in the corner of the backyard where the box is."

"Really?" I couldn't believe it. My heart was thumping away in my chest, making it hard to breathe. "Are you sure you can't see more than that? Could you move to another window?"

"Don't you think I've tried that?" she said. "Anyway, the fact that he's out there with a torch instead of having the whole backyard lit up tells me he's trying to hide something. What do you think we should do?"

"The logical thing is for you to go over there tomorrow to play with Dudley, right?"

"Yes, but I'm scared," Trudy said. "What if Charlie Brown suspects something? I don't think I could cope."

"Why not?"

"Because I might get caught. Then what?"

She had a point.

"I know," I said. "Take your camera watch and get some pictures of whatever it is. You could do that, couldn't you?"

"I suppose so. But I don't have much time."

"Tell you what, Trudy. Just open the box and take a quick shot of whatever's in there. But don't take any risks. I don't want Charlie Brown to catch you."

After we'd hung up, I thought about what I'd said. I really didn't want Charlie Brown to catch her, and it wasn't just because of her camera watch, either. I was starting to think Trudy might be a friend. It was like what I felt for Toad... almost.

Trudy called me the next afternoon.

"I got it!" she said. "There were papers in the box and I took a picture of the top page. Guess what it said?" Her voice was trembling.

"What?" I held my breath.

"It said, 'Top Secret – Codename: Shroud, Government Property, Your Eyes Only', then someone's name. We've got him!"

Chapter 11

Toad and I met Trudy on the way to school and we talked as we walked along together. We thought Charlie Brown would already be safely at work.

"I can't believe what a great weekend it was," Toad said. "Matt, you *talked* to Low Fat, and Trudy got the evidence we needed. We're all set to go."

"I have to get the film developed first," Trudy reminded him. "And I don't have enough money. Have you guys got any?" she asked.

"I've got a dollar," I offered. "It's my drink money, but you can have it."

"I have three or four dollars at home. Will that be enough?" Toad asked.

"Yeah, if I add it to what I have left over from my dog-sitting money. I'll take the film in tomorrow."

We arrived at school and made our way to the classroom. Mrs Larson was at the door, fanning herself. Her eyes were watering.

"Good morning, Mrs Larson," Toad said.

She just nodded.

"Is something wrong?" Trudy asked.

Mrs Larson turned her head towards our room. "The caretaker is on his way," she said.

We went in and were overcome by a really horrible stink.

"What's that awful smell?" I asked Chicken Legs Hunt.

"I don't know. Mrs Larson thinks something must have got into the classroom over the weekend and died."

"It must have been a terrible death," Toad said.

Just then the caretaker arrived. He had rubber gloves on and was holding a plastic bag. We all watched as he went through our room. He opened the cloakroom and looked in every nook and cranny. He found three bags with half-eaten lunches in them. He opened the bags and sniffed inside, but they weren't the problem.

Next, he started walking around the room, sniffing as he went. He stopped at my desk.

Even before he leaned over to look inside, I knew what it was – those chicken parts!

He held the sandwich bag out at arm's length and dropped it into his plastic bag.

Mrs Larson said, "Matt, I'd like an explanation." She had a no-nonsense look on her face.

"It's just some stuff I forgot to take home on Friday. I'm really sorry."

"What kind of stuff?"

"Some chicken."

"Chicken doesn't smell anything like *that*, young man."

I thought I'd better be honest. "Uncooked chicken does."

Mrs Larson just looked at me for a long time. Finally, she said, "I'm not going to ask why you have raw chicken in your desk. I don't think I want to know. Just remember this: If you ever, and I do mean *ever*, bring any kind of bizarre thing to school again, you'll have a detention every day for six months. This is not an idle threat." She began throwing open the windows, and plugged in a fan to blow the stink out.

I looked at Trudy, but I couldn't get her attention. She was flicking through her maths book, avoiding me. I turned towards Toad and he, for once, looked sorry for me. But, as usual, I was the one to get caught.

At lunchtime, Toad and I were sitting together. He had a hot lunch and I had my usual peanut butter-and-jam sandwich with pickles.

"Well, Matt?" Toad asked. "Do you want to swap lunches?"

I eyed the meat and gravy pooled in a pile of mashed potatoes, and chocolate cake on the side. Why does it always look better than it tastes?

"OK," I said, swapping my lunch and sliding Toad's tray in front of me. The first two bites confirmed my suspicions. "You got the best of that deal," I muttered.

Toad smiled happily.

I'll never understand why Toad's mum makes him buy a hot lunch every day when all he ever wants is peanut butter and jam.

"Mind if I sit here?"

I'd know that voice anywhere. It was melodious. (I'd learnt that word in music class.) I turned my head and looked right into Megan Anderson's violet eyes.

"OK," I said, suddenly glad I didn't have peanut butter stuck to the roof of my mouth. The glob of mashed potatoes filling my cheeks was going to be hard enough to swallow.

Megan was smiling. Her teeth sparkled. Her hair shone. The soft pink sweater she was wearing looked like a cloud surrounding her.

"Matt, I've been wondering," her melodious voice began. "Well, it's a bit hard to say, but... I really think you're great. And I'd like to... well, you know..."

Was that a *blush* I saw staining her flawless complexion? Megan Anderson *blushes* when she talks to me? Did I hear her right? Was she saying what I thought she was saying?

I could feel my heart pounding, but I wasn't breathing at all. I vaguely wondered how long somebody could not breathe and still have their heart keep beating.

"Matt, I need to talk to you and Toad. Right now." This voice was definitely not melodious. This voice belonged to Trudy.

"Not now, Trudy," I said, my eyes still riveted to Megan Anderson's face.

"What's up, Trudy?" Toad asked.

"I have to talk to both of you," she said.

I tore my eyes away from the world's most beautiful girl and looked at Trudy.

"Alone," she said, eyeing Megan. "Please."

"Come on, Matt. You're not going to make me leave just so you can talk to Trudy, are you?" Megan's voice had turned to fingernails on a chalkboard.

"It's important, Megan," Trudy said.

"Well, so am I," Megan said nastily. "And I'm very sure Matt prefers to talk to me, don't you, Matt?"

I looked at Megan, then I looked at Trudy.

"It'll only take a minute, Megan. I'll come straight back," I said, getting up.

"You're choosing Trudy over me?" Megan screeched. "Well, forget everything I said before. You're a creep!" She turned to Trudy. "And you're one, too."

Trudy winced. I could tell her feelings were hurt. And it wasn't fair. She didn't deserve it.

"At least she's nice to people!" I yelled at Megan's retreating back. "Come on, Trudy. Let's go outside where we can talk."

We sat under the big tree on the school lawn. I pulled up some grass and tore it into little pieces. I couldn't believe how nasty Megan had been and how easily I had let her go. My insides were all scrambled up, and I didn't really understand how I felt.

There was a warm hand on my arm and I looked up into Trudy's eyes. "I really am sorry, Matt. I know how much you like her."

"I'm glad you know, because I don't."

"Thanks for defending me, though, Matt. I'm really grateful."

"Hey, if you two are going to keep up this mushy stuff, I'm leaving," Toad said.

I punched him in the arm. "What did you have to tell us, Trudy?"

"I've been watching Charlie Brown all week," Trudy began. "He sometimes leaves at night for three or four hours. I know because I see him let Dudley out into the backyard, then all the house lights go out. Then later, all the lights go back on and he lets Dudley in. On Wednesday and Friday nights he leaves about nine o'clock, and he gets back about midnight. He goes out on other nights, too, but only for about half an hour."

"Do you think he's going out to Axion?" Toad asked.

"I'd bet my camera watch on it."

I looked at Toad. I knew he was thinking what I was thinking.

Trudy grinned. She was thinking it, too.

"We'll follow him next Wednesday," I said.

Chapter 12

When Toad and I got to school on Wednesday, Trudy was waiting for us under the big tree.

"I got the pictures back," she said.

We sat down and waited while Trudy unzipped her backpack. I had to laugh when a small blob of plastic explosive rolled out.

"Aren't you creeps friendly," a voice said.

Megan Anderson and Nicole Green were strolling by. They put their heads together and whispered to each other for a moment, then burst out laughing.

"That girl is nasty," Toad muttered.

I watched Megan walk away and wondered how I could have been so wrong about her.

I took the first pictures from Trudy and stared into the face of Low Fat. There was no doubt about his identity. The next picture was of Charlie Brown holding up both mechanical pencils. I quickly flipped through the pictures but there weren't any with both Charlie Brown and Low Fat together.

I wondered if one with Charlie Brown and Low Fat's chest and left arm would be conclusive enough, but I doubted it.

I started going through them again.

Seeing the pictures Trudy took in the conference room at Axion brought it all back. Charlie Brown's face looked dark and angry, not at all the way he looked normally. It was obvious he was talking to someone, but it could have been anyone. I felt really let down. Who would believe he was giving top-secret information to a spy just from these pictures?

"So, what do you think of the pictures?" Trudy asked.

"They don't prove much," I said.

"Look at this. Here's the proof," Toad said, handing me the last of the prints.

My eyes popped at the first picture. Nestled in the buried box was a manila folder secured with rubber bands. In large black letters appeared the words: "Top Secret – Codename: Shroud, Government Property, Your Eyes Only, Hiram Larson."

"Mr Larson! Do you suppose he and Charlie Brown are in this together?" I asked.

"I never thought of that," Toad said slowly. "But, it would explain why he wouldn't listen to us about Charlie Brown."

"Come on, you guys. There is no way Mr Larson is involved," Trudy said.

"How do you know?" I asked.

"I just know, that's all." She looked so defiant I didn't want to cross her, but I wasn't convinced.

"Maybe we'll find out tonight," Toad said, standing up as the first bell rang.

We were surprised to see our day relief teacher, Mrs Murdock. She took our class only when Mrs Larson was away, sick. We didn't like her very much.

Mrs Murdock's favourite word was "detention", and she usually said it while pointing a long skinny finger at the offender. I was usually the offender she was pointing at.

"Where's Mrs Larson?" Toad asked.

"In hospital," Mrs Murdock replied. "Open your maths books at page fifty-six."

I decided that was all the information we were going to get. I leaned down next to my desk and whispered, "Hey, Toad."

"Yeah?"

"Maybe Mrs Larson's got something deadly and Mr Larson had to sell secrets to pay for her care," I whispered, excited by my idea.

"You there, the boy who's half on the floor. Matthew, isn't it?" Mrs Murdock said.

I felt the tips of my ears burning. I *hate* it when anyone calls me Matthew!

"Yes, Mrs Murdock," I said, sitting up.

Her bony finger almost touched my nose. "Detention!"

I heard Megan and Nicole giggling.

So, what's new? I thought.

The phone was ringing when I arrived home after my detention. It was Trudy.

"Matt, you won't believe this! Charlie Brown asked me to watch Dudley again, only this time he doesn't know how long he'll be away. He's left twenty kilograms of dog food!"

"So?"

"That's only part of it. I overheard him talking on the phone. He said, 'This is it. I think someone knows. I'll go to Axion tonight, then meet you at the old cemetery.' We have to stop him tonight, Matt!"

"How are we going to do that?" I croaked.

"No sweat," Trudy said calmly. "There are guards all over the place out there. We just have to convince them he's a spy, that's all."

We met at half past eight. We decided to dress in black so we'd be difficult to see, but our bikes were pretty visible.

It took about twenty minutes to reach Axion. The floodlights made the building look like a concrete bunker.

We parked our bikes and stood there for a minute. I looked at Toad, then Trudy. I couldn't help the grin that spread over my face. We were going to break into the Axion Satellite Corporation!

Chapter 13

"Let's go," I whispered, feeling the adrenalin surging through my body. I was more excited than I was scared.

"Hang on," Trudy said. "We have to work out how to get in."

"She's right," Toad said.

Suddenly two large lights illuminated the trees and bushes around us. The lights danced crazily as we scrambled for cover. It was only a truck backing up to the side of the building. More floodlights went on as the truck stopped, making the loading-bay sign visible.

Two men got out of the truck. There was a telephone on the outside wall of the loading bay. One of the men picked it up and said, "Delivery of computer goods."

After a minute or so, he said, "OK. Ready when you are." Then he hung up.

The men rolled a huge piece of equipment down the ramp, and the door to Axion opened. We watched as they unloaded more equipment, always letting the door close behind them when they went inside the building.

Then they came out and one of the men said, "Only one more after this one, and then we can call it a night."

When the door closed after them, Toad said, "This is our chance! We grab the door before it closes all the way, wait a second, then go in!"

It was really pretty easy. The men carted their last item into Axion, and Toad caught the door before it shut. We waited a moment, then slowly opened the door. There wasn't anyone around, so we set off down a corridor.

Trudy pointed to the foyer sign and we made for that. It led to the reception area where all the trees and plants were. We could see two guards drinking coffee and talking.

We hid in the plants, watching the big steel door with the guards stationed outside it.

"What do you think?" I whispered.

"I think we should sit tight until Charlie Brown comes through that door," Trudy said.

We waited and waited. My legs began to feel numb and I wasn't excited any more. In fact, I was starting to get sleepy.

Just when I thought I'd have to sit down, there was a click and the steel door opened. Standing in the bright light was Charlie Brown.

"You're working late, Mr Brown," one guard said as he looked through the folder Charlie Brown was carrying.

Toad gave a signal to Trudy and me, and we all ran straight towards Charlie Brown. Toad came in on the left, and I came in on the right, but Trudy reached him first.

She grabbed him just as one of the guards pressed a red button that set off blaring alarms all over the building. All the doors locked with a loud click and metal bars slid down, sealing them off.

"What's going on?" Charlie Brown yelled, losing his composure. "Trudy! What are you doing in here?" He looked really dismayed, then he started acting like his cool self again.

"Don't talk to me, you creep!" Trudy spat the words out, then turned to the guard. "Arrest this man. He's a spy!"

"So it was you..." Charlie Brown said, realizing too late that Trudy, who he trusted, was one of the children who had accused him.

By this time there were six guards in a circle around us. The only good thing was that Charlie Brown stood within the circle, too.

"What's going on here?" a deep voice asked. A white-haired man in a military uniform stepped up to Charlie Brown.

"It's nothing, sir." Charlie Brown flashed his big smile. "Some kids got into the building somehow. I'll take care of it."

"Not so fast," the white-haired man said. "How did they get in?"

"I don't know, sir, but I'll sort it out." Charlie Brown flashed another smile.

The white-haired man looked at us for a minute, then nodded to Charlie Brown. "Carry on," he said and started to walk away.

Toad and I looked at each other. We were scared stiff.

As usual, Trudy was one step ahead of us. "Wait a minute. This man's a spy!"

The white-haired man stopped and looked back at us over his shoulder.

"What are you talking about?" Charlie Brown asked Trudy. "I've tried to be nice to you. I've even trusted you with my dog. Whatever gave you the idea that I'm a spy?"

"We have proof," Trudy shouted. "Does the top-secret codename 'Shroud' mean anything to you?"

"Red Alert!" the white-haired man shouted just as Charlie Brown lunged through the ring of guards.

There was complete chaos as the guards wrestled all of us to the floor. I felt my arms being pinned behind my back and saw with horror that both Toad and Trudy had been restrained by guards, too.

It was over in just a few seconds. Charlie Brown lay on the floor, two guards pinning him down. He was looking straight at me. This time, he wasn't smiling.

Toad, Trudy, and I were being held in a small room with security guards blocking the doors. There was a knock, and the white-haired man in the military uniform entered.

"I'm Colonel Westerman. Who are you?" he asked Trudy.

"My name is Trudy Cooper. I'm eighth in our class and I don't have a serial number. That's all you are going to get until I see Mr Hiram Larson."

Colonel Westerman turned to Toad.

"My name is Walter Abernathy, I'm third in our class, and I don't have a serial number, either." Then Toad added, "Nobody calls me Walter except my mum. I'm Toad."

When Colonel Westerman looked at me, I knew just what to say. "My name is Matthew Doyle, but you can call me Matt. I'm seventeenth in our class." I didn't tell him there are only seventeen kids in our class. "And what's a serial number?"

"Stop talking nonsense. This is very serious. You *have* to tell me what all this spy business is about. And you have to tell me *now*!"

"Where is Charlie Brown?" I asked.

The colonel glared at me. "Tell me what this is about and I'll tell you about Mr Brown."

"Call Mr Larson and we'll tell you," I said.

The colonel glared even more, then left.

I breathed a sigh of relief. "Good. He's going to get Mr Larson."

Toad looked at me and said, "That might not be so good. What if Mr Larson's in on it?"

Trudy stuffed her hands in her pockets. She looked first at Toad, then at me. Finally, she said, "He's not. I'm sure he's not."

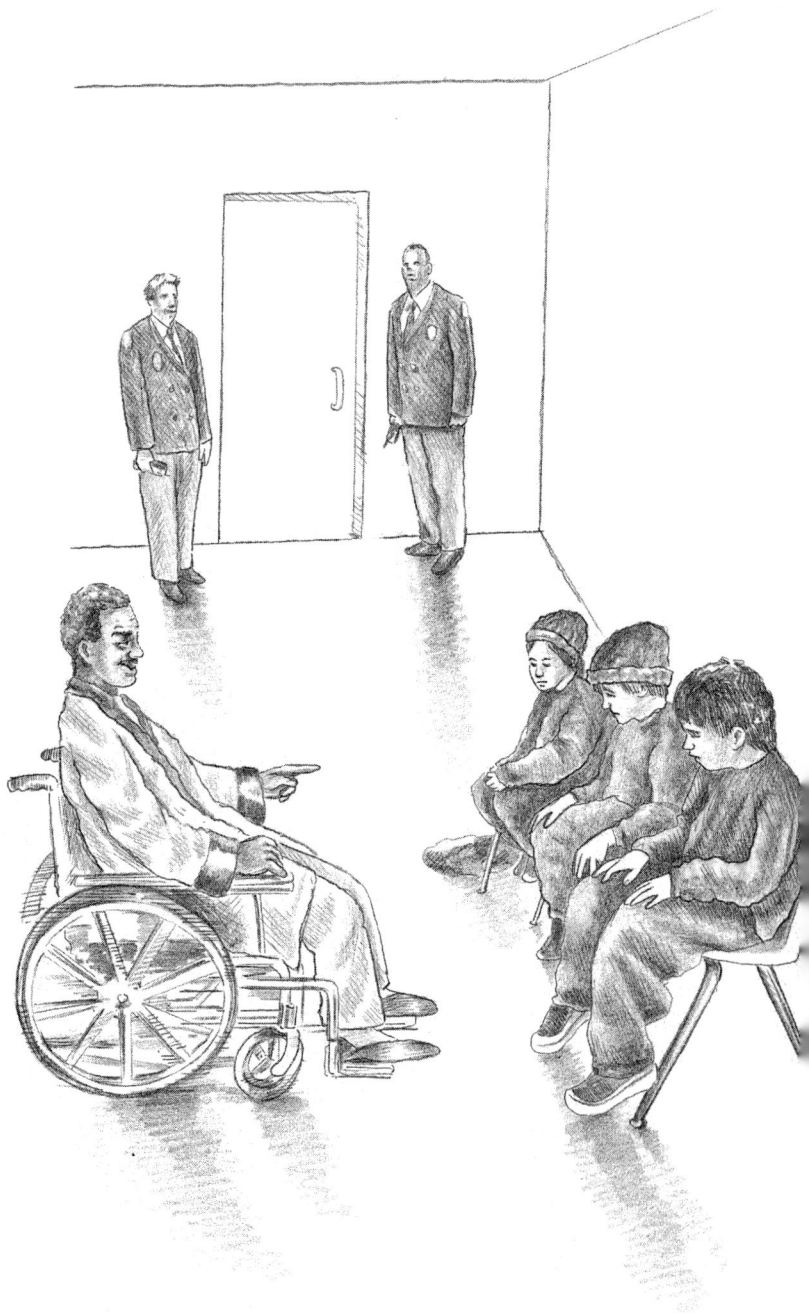

Chapter 14

Mr Larson rolled into the room in his pyjamas and dressing gown. He looked tired and worried.

"You three!" he said. "I should have known it would be you. You tried to cause trouble the day my wife brought your class here. Well, you've really done it now."

"Mr Larson," Trudy spoke softly. "You didn't believe us when we told you Charlie Brown was a spy. But, we have proof now."

He looked at us in complete amazement. "What are you talking about?" he asked.

"I told you before, Charlie Brown is a decent, loyal citizen. They don't come any better."

"Just let them talk, Hiram," Colonel Westerman said.

Trudy put the photos of Charlie Brown and Low Fat on the table.

"This is Charlie Brown's contact," she said. "He poses as a milk-delivery person."

"I've seen him," Mr Larson said. "He delivers for MooTown Dairy. But that certainly doesn't prove the man's a spy!"

"How about this?" Trudy asked, handing him the picture of the contents of the buried metal box.

"Where did you get this?" Mr Larson asked, total disbelief on his face.

We told him.

"I swear that it's locked in my safe," he said.

"It probably is," Toad agreed. "Charlie Brown must have it on microfilm by now."

Mr Larson hung his head, shaking it sadly back and forth. "I had to give him the combination to my safe when my wife first got sick. I trusted him." He looked up at Colonel Westerman. "I just can't believe this," he said.

"The guard went through the papers he was carrying when he came down from his office, tonight. He didn't have anything on him, then," Colonel Westerman said.

"Did you get a chance to check his mechanical pencils?" Trudy asked.

The colonel got up hastily and went out.

"I really trusted him. I really did," Mr Larson said again.

I looked at Toad. "Still think he's involved?"

Toad shook his head. So did Trudy. She was right, once again.

Colonel Westerman walked back in and handed Trudy two mechanical pencils. "These belong to Mr Brown. Is there something special about them?"

All three of us noticed the red band around the top. Trudy pulled the top off and the microfilm fell out.

Mr Larson looked at it dully. "The second half of the Shroud programme came in today. That photograph was of a file containing the first half. It appears he now has the whole system of how to make our satellites invisible."

"But he hasn't passed it on yet," Trudy said brightly. "He's supposed to meet Low Fat at the old cemetery tonight!"

Colonel Westerman scratched something on a pad, then said, "What does this Low Fat look like?"

"Here's his picture," Trudy said.

The colonel looked at the picture, wrote some more, then quickly left the room.

It got really quiet. We all heard Toad swallow, then he coughed to cover it up.

Mr Larson looked miserable. I felt really sorry for him.

"Why is Mrs Larson staying in hospital?" Trudy asked.

Mr Larson lifted his head. "She's having tests done. Did you know that she has cancer?"

Cancer! I had never even thought of that.

"No, we didn't know," Toad said.

"You probably noticed the wig," Mr Larson continued. "She lost all of her hair when she started treatment. Don't look so sad. She's doing well, now. She'll be home tomorrow and back at school on Friday."

He looked at each of us. "Really, she's OK. The doctors think the cancer is under control now. She still gets tired easily, and she's pretty weak. But she's always telling me that you guys give her the will to keep going. She loves teaching, and she always gets lots of laughs in your class." He smiled.

"Is she really OK?" Trudy asked.

"Really, she is," Mr Larson answered with a smile. "And she loves you kids. There's one boy in your room. I forget his name, but he's always getting a detention. Anyway, Mrs Larson tells me he's a great kid. He just always ends up in the wrong place at the right time. He's one of her favourites."

My face was burning. I could feel the hot blush creeping up my neck.

"I shouldn't have told you that," Mr Larson said. "I mean, I'd hate that kid to find out. Mrs Larson would scalp me, then I'd have to wear a wig, too." He began to laugh.

Trudy and Toad laughed. "Don't worry. We won't tell anyone," Toad said, grinning, and looking directly at me.

Half an hour later, Colonel Westerman came back. "Follow me," he said.

I was terrified. Now what? Had we done something wrong, again?

We passed the place in the reception area where Charlie Brown had been captured. The same guards stood at the steel door. It didn't look as though anything at all had happened. Maybe it was all a bad dream.

Colonel Westerman took us into the large conference room. There, on the table, were cups of steaming hot chocolate, a packet of biscuits, and a bowl of apples and bananas.

"Sit down, all of you, and have something to eat," the colonel said.

Toad and Trudy didn't need a second invitation, but I wasn't sure I could get anything past the lump in my throat.

"We owe you kids a big thank you," Colonel Westerman said. "You discovered a brand-new spy ring that we weren't even aware of. We had no idea Charlie Brown was dealing with them. And, even though we check *every* document that comes out of here, he was able to smuggle out that file. And we never thought to check those mechanical pencils. If it weren't for you, we never would have caught him."

Colonel Westerman smiled at me. "As for Charlie Brown, he's being taken to a military prison where he'll await trial for treason."

"What about Low Fat?" Toad asked.

"He was picked up at the cemetery twenty minutes ago," Colonel Westerman said. "He's been talking his head off, so I don't think we'll have trouble getting information out of him."

121

"Good," Mr Larson said.

Toad was grinning from ear to ear. Trudy looked pretty solemn, though.

"What's wrong?" I asked.

Before Trudy could say anything, Colonel Westerman handed her a piece of paper. Trudy read the note and broke into a big smile. "Wow, really?" she said.

"Yes, really," the colonel answered.

"Charlie Brown said Dudley's mine," she said. "He knows I'll take good care of him." She paused, then added, "He says he's sorry."

"He should be," Toad said.

"You kids have to be debriefed," Colonel Westerman said. "Now, eat up that food!"

By Friday morning, everyone at school knew we had caught the spies, and they all wanted to hear the whole story over and over again. I was getting sick of talking about it.

The girls all wanted to be Trudy's best friend. Everyone except Megan and Nicole, that is. But no one was paying much attention to them. I was glad the girls were seeing Trudy through different eyes. I hoped it would last.

Later, as Toad and I were walking in after break, he handed me the stink bomb.

"No way. I'm not touching that thing. Mrs Larson is too nice to have a stink bomb go off in her class."

"Aw, come on. You're not going to turn into a teacher's pet are you?"

Just then, Trudy walked up. "What have you got there?" she asked.

Twenty minutes later, right in the middle of our spelling test, the stink bomb went off.

Mrs Larson marched us outside, just like a fire drill. "All right, who's responsible for this?" she yelled, looking straight at me.

I looked at Toad and said, "He is."

Toad looked at Trudy and said, "She is."

Trudy looked at me and said, "He is."

Mrs Larson looked surprised. "Well, the three of you will have detention for a month for this!"

I just looked at Toad and Trudy, and grinned. At least I wouldn't be in there alone any more!

From the Author

I live in Colorado with my husband and our
English sheepdog, Tillie. The idea for *Follow
That Spy!* came from my husband, who works
at a plant very much like the Axion Satellite
Corporation in the book. However, no plots
have been discovered at his plant!

Ann Sullivan

From the Illustrator

I was born in Toledo, Ohio, in 1954. In addition to illustrating children's books and magazine articles, I enjoy hang-gliding, snowshoeing, and playing bingo.

Ralph Whirly

CONFIDENCE AND
COURAGE
Imagine this, James Robert
Follow That Spy!
Who Will Look Out for Danny?
Fuzz and the Glass Eye
Bald Eagles
Cottle Street

SOMETHING STRANGE
My Father the Mad Professor
A Theft in Time: Timedetectors II
CD and the Giant Cat
Chocolate!
White Elephants and Yellow Jackets
Dream Boat

ANOTHER TIME,
ANOTHER PLACE
Cloudcatcher
Flags
The Dinosaur Connection
Myth or Mystery?
Where Did the Maya Go?
The Journal: Dear Future II

WHEN THINGS GO WRONG
The Long Walk Home
The Trouble with Patrick
The Kids from Quiller's Bend
Laughter is the Best Medicine
Wild Horses
The Sunday Horse

Written by **Ann Sullivan**
Illustrated by **Ralph Whirly**
Edited by **David Nuss**
Designed by **Gary Haney**

09 08 07
11 10 9 8 7

Published in Australia and New Zealand by MIMOSA/McGraw-Hill,
8 Yarra Street, Hawthorn, Victoria 3122, Australia.
Published in the United Kingdom by Kingscourt/McGraw-Hill,
Shoppenhangers Road, Maidenhead, Berkshire SL6 2QL

Printed in China through Colorcraft Ltd., Hong Kong
ISBN 10: 1-57257-741-X
ISBN 13: 978-1-57257-741-1